Animal Lives

ELEPHANTS

Sally Morgan

QED Publishing

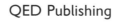

Copyright © QED Publishing 2004

First published in the UK in 2004 by
QED Publishing
A Quarto Group Company
226 City Road
London EC1V 2TT

www.qed-publishing.co.uk

A Catalogue record for this book is
available from the British Library.

ISBN 1 84538 296 X

Written by Sally Morgan
Designed by Tall Tree Books
Editor Christine Harvey
Map by PCGraphics (UK) Ltd

Creative Director Louise Morley
Editorial Manager Jean Coppendale

Printed and bound in China

Picture credits

Key: t = top, b = bottom, m = middle,
c = centre, l = left, r = right

Ecoscene /Kjell Sandved 5tr, /Papilio /R
Pickett 6, /Neeraj Mishra 10, 30tl, /Karl
Ammann 11t, 27tr, 30tr, /Sally Morgan 15,
30br, /Luc Hosten 22, 28bl, /Papilio /
Robert Gill 26, /Stephen Coyne 29
Getty Images front cover Jonathan &
Angela, /Jack Hollingsworth 4–5, 30bl,
/Johnny Johnson 7, /K Begg 8–9, /Art Wolfe
11b, 24–25, /Stan Osolinski 12–13, /Johan
Elzenga 14, 17, /Pascal Crapet 16, /Harald
Sund 1, 18–19, /Daryl Balfour 20, /Renee
Lynn 21, /Tim Davis 23bl, 23tr /Gavriel Jecan
24bl, /Douglas-Hamilton 28tr

The words in **bold** are
explained in the Glossary
on page 31.

Contents

The elephant

The elephant has a huge grey body and strong legs that look like pillars. It has a long **trunk** instead of the short nose that we have. It also has large flapping ears. Most elephants have **tusks**, too. These are extra long teeth, which continue to grow throughout the elephant's life. The male elephant is called a bull and the female is called a cow. Elephants live in groups called herds.

A fully grown female elephant uses her trunk to feed on grass.

What sort of animal is an elephant?

The elephant belongs to a group of animals called **mammals**. Other mammals include lions, horses and humans.

An elephant's tusks grow up to 18cm a year.

Elephant

The elephant is the largest living land animal.

fact

Elephant types

There are three species, or types, of elephant. They are the African, African forest and Asian elephants. The Asian elephant is often called the Indian elephant.

The African elephant is the largest of the elephants. It has large ears and long tusks. The Asian elephant has much smaller ears and its skin is less wrinkled.

An Asian female elephant. The Asian elephant has small ears and a long face.

Spot the difference

Look quickly and you may think the African and African forest elephants appear the same. But there are some differences. The African forest elephant is smaller. It also has a hairy trunk. Its tusks point downwards so that they do not get tangled up in the **vegetation** in the forests where it lives.

Elephant

- Both the African bull and female elephants have tusks, but only the Asian bull elephant has tusks.

- The African elephant has a dip in its back. The Asian elephant has an arched back.

facts

An African bull elephant.

Where do you find elephants?

The African and African forest elephants live in Africa. The African elephant is found mainly in East Africa, on tropical grassland known as **savannah**. The savannah is a vast open plain covered in grass and a few trees.

The African forest elephant is found in the **tropical forests** of Central and West Africa.

Elephant fact

The African forest elephant is difficult to spot in the forest, so much less is known about it.

African forest elephants in a tropical forest.

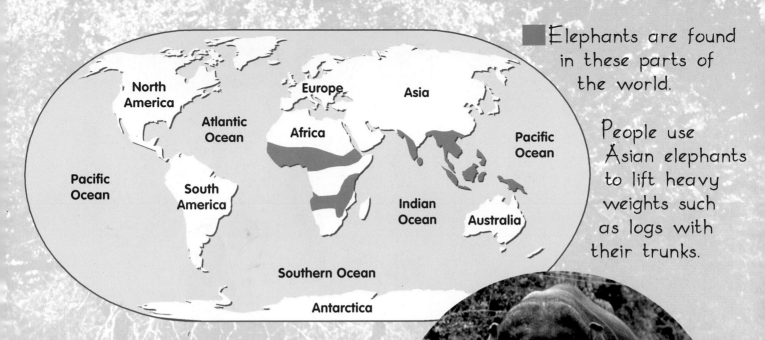

Elephants are found in these parts of the world.

People use Asian elephants to lift heavy weights such as logs with their trunks.

The Asian Elephant

The Asian elephant is found across South and South East Asia. It lives on grassland and in forests.
The Asian elephant has become domesticated. This means it has been captured and kept by humans for thousands of years.

9

Beginning life

After mating with a bull elephant, a female elephant is **pregnant** for 22 months. She gives birth to only one baby at a time. A baby elephant is called a calf. A newborn calf has gingery hair over its head and back. It gradually loses this hair as it gets older.

The calf feeds on its mother's milk for the first three years of its life. Then it starts to eat grass and other plants. It also has to learn how to behave around the adult members of the herd.

An Asian elephant calf with its mother.

Elephant

A newborn elephant calf weighs between 77 and 113kg. It stands about 90cm high from the ground to its shoulder.

fact

A special day

The birth of a baby elephant is a special day for the herd. All the elephants crowd around the mother to touch her new calf. The elephants are very excited and make a lot of noise.

An elephant calf will drink up to 11 litres of its mother's milk every day.

An elephant calf exploring its habitat.

Having calves

A female elephant is old enough to have a calf when she is about 17 years old. She will have six or seven calves during her lifetime. She stops mating when she reaches 50 years of age.

Growing up

A female elephant usually has several youngsters with her, ranging in age from a few months to ten years. Young calves are protected by the herd. If the mother dies, the other elephants look after her young.

Growing bigger

The calf becomes an **adolescent** elephant once it stops drinking its mother's milk at about three years of age. By this time it has teeth, which means it can eat plant food. It has also learned to use its trunk to find food.

Female elephants keep growing until they are about 20 years of age. They do not grow much after this. Bull elephants, however, continue to grow until they are about 30 years old.

Elephant facts

- An African elephant weighs about 1000kg by the time it is six years old.

- About half of all elephants die before they reach the age of 15.

Young elephants stay with their mother for the first eight to ten years.

13

Living in a herd

Female elephants live in family groups called herds. A typical herd is made up of three or four adult females and their calves of different ages. All the adult females are related. The herd is led by the oldest female. She is called the matriarch. The herd gets larger as more calves are born, so some of the females may leave and form their own herd.

Young elephants learn by watching their mothers and the other members of the herd.

Bull elephants

While they are growing up in the herd, the young bulls play together. They charge at each other and make a lot of noise. When they leave the herd, they live on their own or join other males. The adult bulls only rejoin the herd when a female is ready to mate. Then they go off on their own again.

Young bull elephants play-fight with each other.

Elephant fact

Sometimes herds join up to form a large family group that may have more than 200 elephants in it.

Young bull elephants leave the herd at around 13 to 15 years of age.

Feeding

Once elephant calves stop taking milk from their mother, they become plant eaters, or herbivores. This happens when calves are about three. Once they start to eat plants, elephants use their trunks to reach food. They also use their trunks to feed from the ground. The adults help the younger elephants to feed by pulling down branches for them.

An elephant's trunk is long enough to reach up into trees for leaves and fruits.

Using their tusks

Elephants use their tusks to dig for food and to pull down trees. Calves have tiny milk tusks which are only 5 to 6cm long. These drop out before the calf reaches two years of age and are replaced by permanent tusks. A tusk grows from a small tooth at the front of the elephant's mouth. It is made of **ivory**.

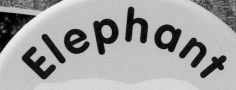

Elephant

Every day an adult elephant eats more than 150kg of food – that is the combined weight of two men!

fact

What do elephants eat?

During the rainy months elephants eat mostly grass. During the dry months they eat shrubs, twigs and bark. They eat flowers, fruits and roots all year round.

As they grow older, the young elephants have to learn what is good to eat and what they should avoid.

17

Teeth

Elephants use their teeth for grinding plant food. They break the food down into small pieces and then they swallow it. Calves are born with four large teeth that are flat. New teeth form in the back of the mouth and push the old ones out.

Elephants eat grass, leaves, roots and fruits. They use their tusks to peel the bark off trees.

The elephant moves its jaws from side to side, grinding the grass between its teeth.

Adult teeth

An elephant usually grows six sets of teeth in its lifetime. The final set appear when it is about 40 years old. These are the largest teeth and each is 21cm long and weighs 4kg! An elephant's teeth wear down as it gets older. Once its teeth are worn away an elephant cannot chew any more, so it dies from starvation.

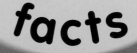

Elephant facts

- An elephant's tooth is the largest tooth produced by any mammal.

- The life span of an elephant is about 70 years.

Trunks

An elephant uses its trunk to smell. The trunk is formed from the elephant's nose and upper lip. There are two nostrils that run down the whole trunk. Smell helps to keep the herd together. It allows elephants to detect predators, such as lions or tigers. At the first hint of danger, an elephant raises its trunk to smell the air. Smell also helps elephants to find food and water.

Elephants can pick up very small objects with the end of their trunks, in the same way that we use our fingertips.

How do elephants use their trunks?

When a calf is about four months old it starts to use its trunk. It has to learn how to move its trunk, just like a human baby has to learn to walk. At first the trunk just hangs down. The calf learns how to use the different muscles to control movement.

Elephants also use their trunks to explore their surroundings. The end of the trunk is very sensitive to touch. It has finger-like flaps at the end.

Elephants rely on their trunks to sense danger in the air.

Elephant fact

The trunk plays such an important part in an elephant's life, that it is almost impossible for an elephant to survive if its trunk is damaged.

Communicating

Elephants, like humans, use different senses to communicate with each other. Elephants make rumbling sounds to talk to each other that we cannot hear. They make these sounds with the voice box in their throat. These rumbles can be heard by other elephants as far as 9km away. Most elephant talk takes place during the afternoon.

Elephants use more than 70 kinds of sounds and 160 different signals in their daily lives.

Elephants greet each other by touching with their trunks.

Elephant noises

Elephants make a trumpeting sound with their **trunks** when they are excited, surprised or when they are about to attack. They also squeal, cry, scream, roar, snort and groan! As they get older elephant calves learn to make all these different sounds. As their body gets bigger and their trunk gets longer, they are able to make louder sounds.

Elephants use signals, such as a raised trunk, to show anger.

Adult signals

Adult elephants flap their ears or raise their trunk and tail to communicate with each other. These are warnings to other animals that the elephant is angry. Touch is important, too. Elephants of all ages touch each other with their trunk when they meet.

Female elephants touch their calves a lot.

Moving

Elephants are such large animals that they need a strong skeleton to support their body. Elephants normally have 20 ribs which form a huge barrel-shaped ribcage. Around their bones are muscles. Muscles are attached to bones and when they **contract** they pull on the bone to make it move.

Elephants can run faster than humans.

Walking, running – and sliding!

Elephants can walk and run, but they cannot leap or jump like many other mammals. They walk at speeds of up to 13km per hour. To walk faster they take longer, quicker strides. Sometimes elephants climb up slopes, or slide down them. Elephants can walk almost silently because they have a spongy cushion on the bottom of their feet, which muffles any noise.

Elephant

- A charging elephant runs at 40km per hour.

- The skull of an adult elephant is massive. It can make up as much as one quarter of the elephant's weigh.

facts

Keeping cool

Elephants live in hot climates. Their large bodies heat up in the sun, so they often need to cool down. One way they do this is by visiting water holes or rivers and having a swim. Elephants spend hours resting by water. The calves like to throw water over each other.

Elephants also love to wallow in mud. A covering of mud helps to protect their skin. It acts like sun block, which is what we use to protect our skin from the sun.

Elephants keep cool by spraying water over themselves with their trunks.

Elephant
Elephants flap their ears to stay cool. When elephants flap their ears they lose heat to the surrounding air.
fact

Finding shade

During the hottest part of the day, elephants stand in the shade to stay cool. A calf elephant's skin is very sensitive to the sun. The mother elephant stands over her calves and young to shade them. As an elephant gets older, its skin gets thicker.

Elephants protect themselves from the sun by finding shade from trees.

Elephants in danger

Sadly, the number of elephants in the world has fallen. African elephants have been killed by humans for their ivory tusks. Ivory is valuable to humans. It is used to make ornaments and jewellery. During the 1970s and 1980s thousands of elephants were killed. In 1989 there was a ban on the sale of ivory. Now most elephants are protected.

African elephants were killed for their ivory tusks.

Elephants are protected in national parks.

Protecting elephants

Elephants are suffering because their **habitat** is being damaged. Forest trees are cut down for timber. Grasslands are used for grazing cattle and growing crops. There is less food and space for the elephants.

Today, most wild elephants are found in national parks. These are places where the elephants are protected. Tourists can drive around the parks and see the elephants.

Many Asian elephants work in the timber industry. An adult elephant can drag about half its own weight.

Elephant fact

There are about 600 000 African elephants and 50 000 Asian elephants in the world.

Life cycle

A female elephant is pregnant for 22 months. She gives birth to a single calf. Young elephants drink their mothers' milk for 3 years. They stay close to their mother for 10 years. Young males leave the herd once they reach 13 to 15 years of age. The female elephants stay with the herd. Elephants live to about 70 years of age.

A newborn calf

A 3-year old calf

A 15-year-old bull elephant

An adult cow elephant

Glossary

adolescent the stage in growing up between childhood and adulthood

contract to get shorter

habitat the place where an animal, or a plant lives

ivory the hard white substance that makes up the tusk of an elephant

mammal a warm-blooded animal with a backbone. Mammals give birth to live young, rather than laying eggs. The female mammal produces milk for her young

pregnant a female animal that has a baby developing inside her

savannah a grassy plain with few trees, found in tropical parts of the world, for example East and Southern Africa

tropical forest many trees growing close together in areas near the Equator where the climate is hot and wet for much of the year

trunk the very long nose of the elephant

tusk a long pointed tooth that sticks out of the elephant's mouth

vegetation plant life

Index